W9-AQZ-851

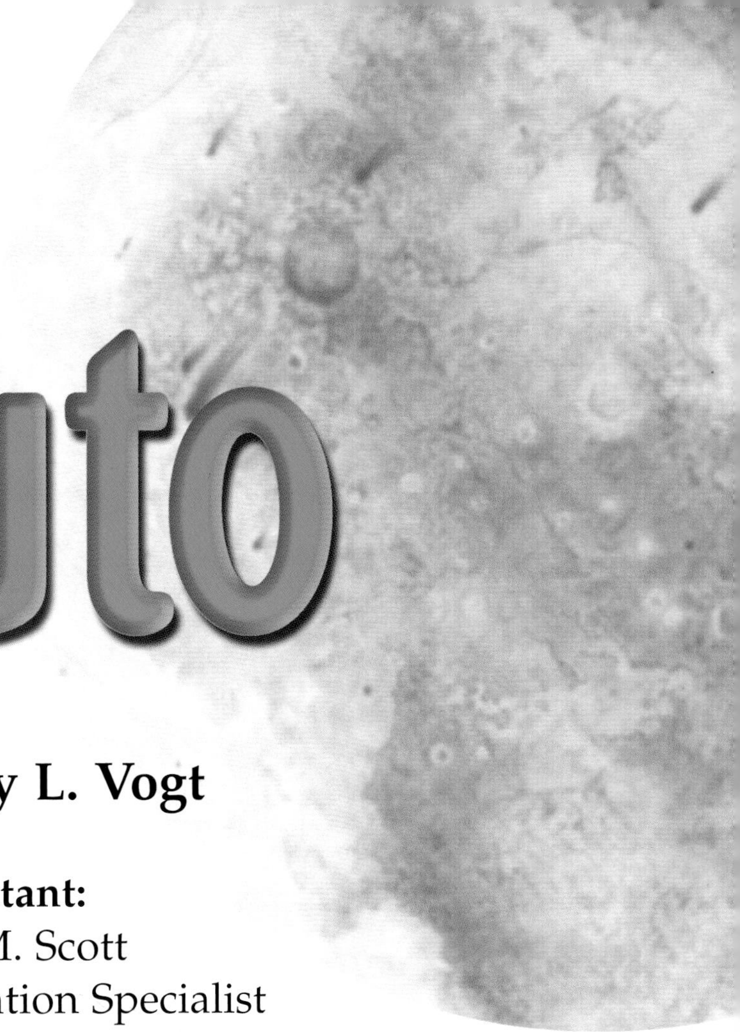

Pluto

by Gregory L. Vogt

Consultant:
Donald M. Scott
Aerospace Education Specialist
Oklahoma State University and
NASA Ames Research Center

Bridgestone Books
an imprint of Capstone Press
Mankato, Minnesota

Bridgestone Books are published by Capstone Press
151 Good Counsel Drive, P.O. Box 669, Mankato, Minnesota 56002
http://www.capstone-press.com

Library of Congress Cataloging-in-Publication Data
Vogt, Gregory.
    Pluto/by Gregory L. Vogt.
    p. cm.—(The galaxy)
    Includes bibliographical references and index.
    Summary: Discusses the surface features, atmosphere, orbit, moon, discovery, and
exploration of the planet Pluto.
    ISBN 0-7368-0514-1
    1. Pluto (Planet)—Juvenile literature. [1. Pluto (Planet)] I. Title. II. Series.
QB701 .V64 2000
523.48'2—dc21
                      99-051640
                         CIP

Editorial Credits
Tom Adamson, editor; Timothy Halldin, cover designer and illustrator; Kimberly Danger
    and Jodi Theisen, photo researchers

Photo Credits
Alan Stern (Southwest Research Institute), Marc Buie (Lowell Observatory), NASA and
    ESA, 12
Courtesy of NASA/JPL/Caltech, 20
Dr. R. Albrecht, ESA/ESO Space Telescope European Coordinating Facility, NASA, 8
Lowell Observatory Photograph, 6
NASA, cover, 1, 10, 16, 18
Nordic Optical Telescope, La Palma, 17
U.S. Naval Observatory, 14

1 2 3 4 5 6 05 04 03 02 01 00

Table of Contents

Relative size of the Sun and the planets

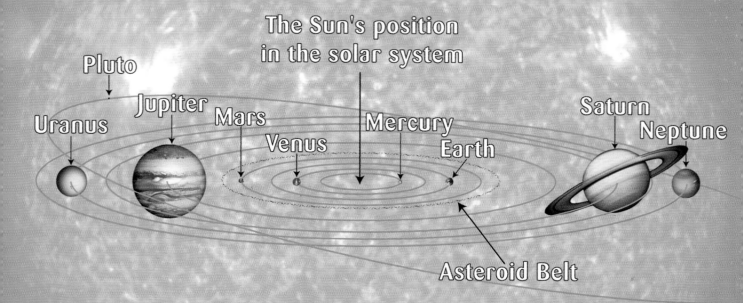

Pluto

Uranus

Jupiter

Mars

Venus

The Sun's position in the solar system

Mercury

Earth

Saturn

Neptune

Asteroid Belt

The Sun

Pluto and the Solar System

Pluto is a planet in the solar system. The Sun is the center of the solar system. Planets, asteroids, and comets travel around the Sun.

Nine known planets move around the Sun. The rocky inner planets are Mercury, Venus, Earth, and Mars. Jupiter, Saturn, Uranus, and Neptune are made of gases. These outer planets are much larger than the inner planets.

Pluto usually is the farthest planet from the Sun. Pluto receives little light or heat from the Sun. This cold planet is probably covered with ice. Scientists have been unable to study the planet in detail. Pluto is too far away to get a clear telescope picture from Earth.

This illustration compares the sizes of the planets and the Sun. Pluto is the smallest planet in the solar system. The blue lines show the orbits of the planets. Thousands of asteroids move around the Sun. The asteroid belt is between the orbits of Mars and Jupiter.

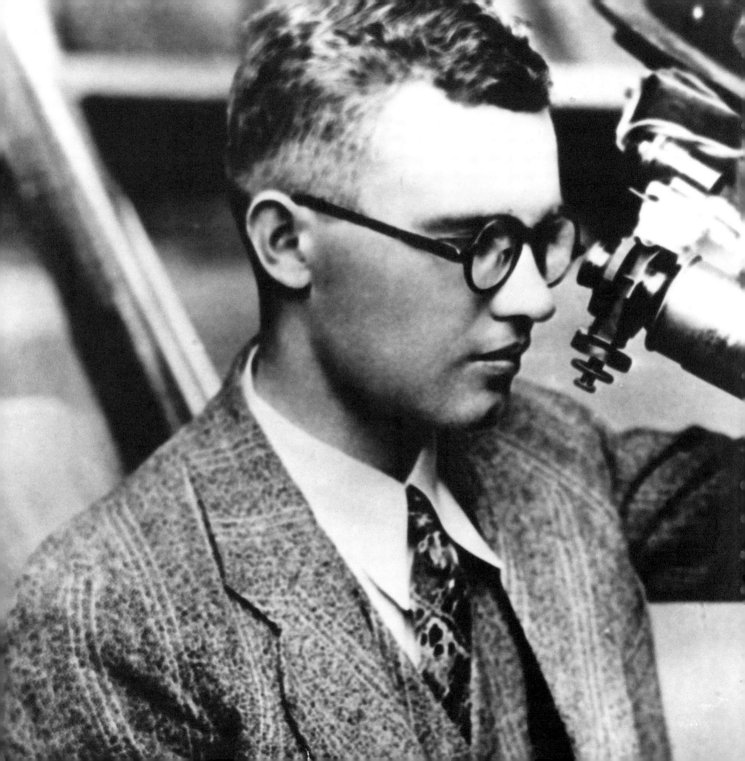

The Planet Pluto

Pluto is the smallest planet in the solar system. At a width of about 1,417 miles (2,280 kilometers), Pluto is even smaller than Earth's Moon.

Pluto is difficult to see from Earth because it is small and far away. Pluto looks like a very faint star, even through a big telescope. Astronomers must know exactly where to look to find Pluto.

In 1930, a young astronomer named Clyde Tombaugh discovered Pluto. Tombaugh used a big telescope to take pictures of the stars. Several days later, he took the same pictures again. Tombaugh compared the pictures. He saw that one star had moved. The movement meant that it was not a star. The object was actually a planet orbiting the Sun.

All the planets except Earth are named for characters in Greek and Roman myths. Pluto was named for the Roman god of the underworld. Venetia Burney, an 11-year-old girl from England, originally suggested the name Pluto.

Clyde Tombaugh was 24 years old when he discovered the planet Pluto in 1930.

FAST FACTS

	Pluto	Earth
Diameter:	1,417 miles (2,280 kilometers)	7,927 miles (12,756 kilometers)
Average distance from the Sun:	3,673 million miles (5,911 million kilometers)	93 million miles (150 million kilometers)
Revolution period:	248 years	365 days, 6 hours
Rotation period:	6 days, 9 hours, 18 minutes	23 hours, 56 minutes
Moons:	1	1

Revolution and Rotation

Like all planets in the solar system, Pluto revolves around the Sun. Planets follow a path called an orbit. Pluto orbits the Sun once about every 248 years.

The Sun's gravity keeps the planets in their orbits. This force pulls objects together. Pluto is the slowest moving planet. It moves slower than the other planets because it is so far from the Sun. The Sun's gravity does not pull Pluto with as much force.

Pluto's orbit is egg-shaped. The planet's distance from the Sun changes as it follows this orbit. When Pluto is farthest from the Sun, it is about 4,500 million miles (7,242 million kilometers) away. When Pluto is closest to the Sun, it is about 2,700 million miles (4,345 million kilometers) away. Between 1979 and 1999, Pluto actually was closer to the Sun than Neptune.

Pluto also rotates, or spins, as it orbits. The planet rotates once every 6 days, 9 hours, and 18 minutes.

Pluto was about 2,600 million miles (4,200 million kilometers) from Earth when the Hubble Space Telescope took this picture.

Most planets are surrounded by a mixture of gases called an atmosphere. Scientists think Pluto's atmosphere is made mostly of nitrogen. Most of the time, the nitrogen is frozen into ice. It depends on Pluto's distance from the Sun.

Pluto becomes very cold as its orbit takes it farther away from the Sun. The atmosphere freezes. The frozen nitrogen falls to the surface of Pluto. The nitrogen ice covers the planet in a layer of frost.

Pluto receives more sunlight when it is closer to the Sun. The sunlight slightly warms the nitrogen ice. Some of the nitrogen ice melts and becomes a gas. Pluto's nitrogen gas and other gases form a thin atmosphere around Pluto.

This painting of Pluto shows how the planet's atmosphere may look.

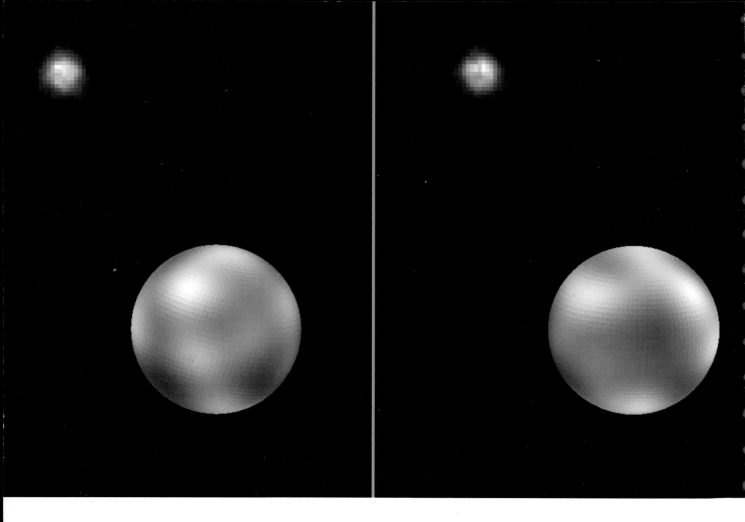

The Hubble Space Telescope took these pictures of Pluto. The two smaller pictures at the top are the actual images from the Hubble. Scientists created the larger pictures with computers. In these larger pictures, they can see Pluto's surface better. Pluto was about 3,000 million miles (4,828 million kilometers) from Earth when the Hubble took the pictures.

The Surface of Pluto

Scientists know little about the surface of Pluto. Pluto's small size and great distance from Earth make it difficult to see. The best telescope pictures of Pluto show the planet as a fuzzy ball. Astronomers have made some discoveries by carefully studying the pictures.

Pluto has light-colored polar caps made of nitrogen ice. Scientists know that it must be very cold on Pluto for nitrogen to change into ice. The temperature on Pluto probably averages minus 400 degrees Fahrenheit (minus 240 degrees Celsius). The polar caps probably shrink when Pluto is nearest the Sun. The caps grow as Pluto travels farther from the Sun.

Astronomers have noticed some features on Pluto that they cannot explain. Pictures show bright areas around the middle of Pluto. Scientists also have seen a stripe that crosses the planet's surface.

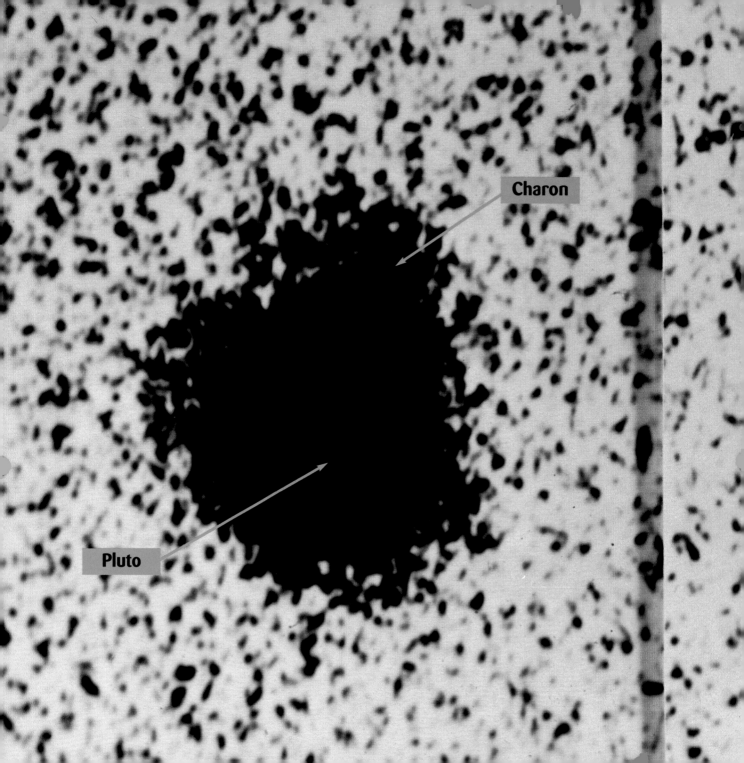

Pluto's Moon

Pluto has one moon called Charon. Charon is 732 miles (1,178 kilometers) wide. Pluto is only 1,417 miles (2,280 kilometers) wide. Charon is about half the size of Pluto. No other moon is this large in comparison to its planet. Some astronomers think of Pluto and Charon as a double planet.

Charon orbits Pluto at a distance of about 12,200 miles (19,630 kilometers). Charon orbits Pluto in 6 days, 9 hours, and 18 minutes. Pluto rotates once in the same amount of time. This means that Charon stays on the same side of Pluto at all times.

James Christy discovered Charon in 1978. He studied a picture of Pluto and noticed a bump on the planet. Other astronomers thought the bump was a flaw in the picture. Christy studied other pictures. The bump was in different places. Christy realized that the bump was a moon. He named the moon Charon.

This telescope photo of Pluto shows a bump. The bump is Pluto's moon, Charon.

Pluto and Charon are cold because they are so far from the Sun.

Scientists believe that both Pluto and Charon are made of rock and nitrogen ice. Small amounts of frozen methane and carbon monoxide are mixed in with the nitrogen.

Astronomers do not know if Pluto and Charon are more ice or more rock. The cores of the planet and the moon are probably rock. Ice makes up the surface.

Astronomers do not know what the surfaces of Pluto and Charon look like. They could be smooth. They could be covered with craters.

This photo of Pluto and Charon was taken by the Nordic Optical Telescope. The photo is the best image of Pluto taken by a telescope on the ground.

17

Percival Lowell was an astronomer who lived in the 1800s. He predicted that there was a ninth planet in the solar system. Clyde Tombaugh discovered Pluto after Lowell had died. Pluto's symbol contains Lowell's initials, "PL."

A Planet or an Asteroid?

Some astronomers think that Pluto should not be called a planet. They argue that Pluto is not like other planets. The inner planets are made of rock. The outer planets are made of gases. Pluto is rock and ice. Pluto is smaller than many moons in the solar system. Pluto's orbit also is different from the other planets' orbits.

Some astronomers want Pluto classified as an asteroid. Many of these space rocks are metal. Some asteroids are the size of a house. Others are up to 620 miles (1,000 kilometers) across.

Other astronomers point out that Pluto is much larger than any known asteroids. And unlike asteroids, Pluto has an atmosphere. Most asteroids are shaped like lumpy potatoes. Pluto is round. The two groups of astronomers have not come to an agreement.

This photo of Pluto and Charon was taken by the Hubble Space Telescope.

Exploring Pluto

Space probes from Earth have explored every planet except Pluto. Everything astronomers know about Pluto comes from telescopes.

The best pictures of Pluto come from the Hubble Space Telescope. This huge telescope is in orbit above Earth. Even with this telescope's best pictures, scientists can only guess what Pluto looks like.

Astronomers hope to send a new space probe to Pluto and Charon. The space probe would need 8 to 10 years to travel there. It would send pictures and information about Pluto and Charon back to Earth over radio waves. The space probe then would continue into deep space to study the solar system beyond Pluto. Scientists hope to discover more about the solar system with this mission.

This computer graphic shows what Pluto and Charon might look like.

Hands On: Comparing Distance

Pluto usually is the farthest planet from the Sun. You can make a model of the solar system. The model will show you how far Pluto is from the Sun and the other planets.

What You Need

Nine sticks at least 1 foot
    (30 centimeters) long
Strips of colorful fabric
Tape
Beach ball
Yard stick or meter stick
Football field or park

Distance from the Sun		
Planet	**U.S.**	**Metric**
Mercury	1 foot	30 centimeters
Venus	2 feet	61 centimeters
Earth	3 feet	91 centimeters
Mars	4.5 feet	1.4 meters
Jupiter	5 yards	4.6 meters
Saturn	9.5 yards	8.7 meters
Uranus	19 yards	17.4 meters
Neptune	30 yards	27.4 meters
Pluto	39.5 yards	36.1 meters

What You Do

1. Tape one strip of fabric to one end of each stick to make nine flags.
2. Place the beach ball on the ground. The ball represents the Sun.
3. Measure 1 foot (30 centimeters) from the Sun. Place a flag in the ground. This flag represents the planet Mercury.
4. Measure 2 feet (61 centimeters) from the Sun. Place another flag in the ground. This flag represents Venus.
5. Continue with the other planets according to the above chart.

In your model, 1 yard (91 centimeters) equals 93 million miles (150 million kilometers). Astronomers call this distance 1 Astronomical Unit (AU). Pluto is about 39.5 AU from the Sun. A space probe from Earth would take about 8 to 10 years to get to Pluto.

Words to Know

asteroid (ASS-tuh-roid)—a large space rock that orbits the Sun

astronomer (uh-STRON-uh-mer)—a person who studies planets, stars, and space

gravity (GRAV-uh-tee)—a force that pulls objects together

orbit (OR-bit)—the path of an object as it travels around another object in space

revolution (rev-uh-LOO-shuhn)—the movement of one object around another object in space

rotation (roh-TAY-shuhn)—one complete spin of an object in space

space probe (SPAYSS PROHB)—a spacecraft that travels to other planets and outer space

telescope (TEL-uh-skope)—an instrument that makes faraway objects appear larger and closer

Read More

Brimner, Larry Dane. *Pluto.* A True Book. New York: Children's Press, 1999.

Kerrod, Robin. *Astronomy.* Young Scientist Concepts and Projects. Milwaukee: Gareth Stevens, 1998.

Wetterer, Margaret K. *Clyde Tombaugh and the Search for Planet X.* Minneapolis: Carolrhoda Books, 1996.

Useful Addresses

Canadian Space Agency
6767 Route de l'Aéroport
Saint-Hubert, QC J3Y 8Y9
Canada

Lowell Observatory
1400 West Mars Hill Road
Flagstaff, AZ 86001

NASA Headquarters
Washington, DC 20546-0001

Internet Sites

NASA/JPL Outer Planets/Solar Probe Project
http://www.jpl.nasa.gov/ice_fire
The Nine Planets
http://www.tcsn.net/afiner
StarChild
http://starchild.gsfc.nasa.gov/docs/StarChild/
    StarChild.html

Index